The Heroic Self

The HEROIC SELF

By Patricia Gagné

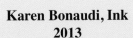

Karen Bonaudi, Ink
2013

The Heroic Self

Copyright ©2013 by Patricia Gagné

Published by Karen Bonaudi, Ink

www.karenbonaudi.com

Printed in the United States of America

ISBN: 978-0-9891430-0-4

Credits

Cover art by H. Lee Shapiro

Photographs by Patricia Gagné

Book design and layout by Poouster Graphics

Web design and construction by Poouster Graphics

www.theheroicself.com/blog

First printing 2013

Preface

I believe that we have the capacity to heal our inner selves by drawing on the healthy energy intrinsic to our being. The grace and harmony of a peaceful spirit is in our nature. The ideas, imagery and poetry in this book are designed to help us as we meet life's challenges. They remind us of the power within and of our ability to draw upon it to lead the lives we desire.

Most of us have a sense of spiritual resources within ourselves. We have turned to prayer, connecting our inner spirit with a higher power. We have sensed the healing power of a place of worship, a community of worshippers, the power of ritual. Many have used yoga and meditation to connect with their deepest selves. The difficulty lies in learning to make the connection between our spiritual resources and our daily lives day by day, hour by hour, as we live our lives.

This book presents a vision of life where our innermost self is our greatest strength. The potential for healing and creative growth lie at the heart of our being. We can heal our hurts and let our lives reflect the beauty and harmony within.

Patricia Gagné

Dedication

For Sam Ronnie
who has never ceased
to be an inspiration in my life

Table of Contents

1 **The Heroic Self**

The great heroic quality of life is the ability to choose what we will be in spite of any obstacle from within or without. Once we are in control of our lives, we will inevitably choose what is best. Only the confused and damaged spirit moves toward what is harmful to itself or to others. The greatness of the human spirit lies in developing the consciousness that empowers us to see clearly, make wise choices, and direct our lives toward what is good.

How do we know that people who are in control of their minds and actions will necessarily turn toward the good? Because the good is constructive. For example, children who are given a set of building blocks normally want to build something with them. But the child who is angry is more likely to smash what has taken hours to create and then cry for the loss. Such a consciousness is "out of control" and has acted against its own interest. Adults follow the same pattern. People in a room with a book or magazine normally look at it to see what it has of interest for them. Only a confused and disoriented mind starts by tearing it up. It is instinctive for people to do what is in their own interest, what is good for them, as long as their choices are guided by a harmony with their true nature.

Yet we are discussing the "heroic quality" of choice. Why would it be heroic for a person to do what comes naturally? Because the nature of the world around us makes it unavoidable that we sometimes become confused, make mistakes, even enjoy acting destructively. Often it feels easier to give ourselves over to negative thoughts and feelings than to try to set matters straight, clarify what the real issues are, and seek the truth.

The heroic quality is a disciplined effort to develop a consciousness that is able to see clearly. Each day of our lives we make decisions about how to react, how to behave or to react to the events of our lives. When others appear unreasonable, do we let anger dominate and retaliate swiftly? Or do we let good sense prevail and think of the best way to handle the situation? Heroes will choose their reaction. Each response based in truth, which is the good of all, strengthens our ability to live well.

The capacity to be heroes is in the nature of all of us. But we must reach for the heroic quality every day, choosing the thoughts, emotions and actions that lead to our own good and to that of the world around us.

AFFIRMATION

I live in a universe which creates instinctive longings for goodness, truth and the well-being of all mankind. I have the power to bring these qualities into my life.

Knowledge of right action and the courage to follow through on such clear thought lie within me. As I turn to that source of wisdom, the good decisions I make bring me closer to the power for good in my life.

True desire and sincere effort join with the natural wisdom and goodness within me. I can develop the heroic spirit and the fulfilled life of my dreams.

The Heroic Self

What if it should rain
in torrents
and the nourishing force
could crush
what struggles to grow,
like new spring buds
in a land of revolution?

What if I can never be
what I want
and trying play the fool
giving so much to care
like a loveless child
still believing in life?

And then the child grew
to cultivate beds of roses?

② The Harmonies of Life

There are natural harmonies in the universe. What is within us patterns the external realities of our existence, creating a correspondence between our internal and external selves. There can be only temporary conflict between the nature of our consciousness and the way in which our lives are lived. Our minds will make our lives what we think they should be.

Many people misunderstand this universal law of correspondence. They believe that when there is calm and ease in their external lives, they will experience a resultant peaceful state in their hearts. Thus they wait for things to go well so that they can enjoy life. It is true that internal and external peace are related. But the central point to understand is that it is the internal, the mind, which creates the external, the world around us.

To understand how our minds create the nature of our existence, let us consider the joy parents so often take in observing a sleeping child. The pleasure of it comes from within. While a joyful heart fills the experience with peace, a heart filled with fear might experience anxiety in such a situation, imagining all the possible harm that might come to this beautiful creature. Our experience mirrors our consciousness. The warmth and comfort of family life is a reflection of the love we hold in our hearts.

In the same way, minds not at peace with themselves create conflict. There would be no war, no family feuds, no heated arguments without angry minds. Most people agree that conflicts are caused by certain individuals who are motivated by anger and fear. But they believe that most of us, far from causing the problem, merely suffer from situations others have created. Few accept responsibility for the role of their own negative thinking in creating the problems in their lives.

Yet the realities of all experience arise from within. For example, to one individual war might represent an opportunity to reflect the hate in his heart by taking advantage of wartime to hurt others. To another it might mean courage in maintaining the safety of fellow citizens. To a third, it might mean learning and new opportunities for growth. The internal realities of each individual largely determine the nature of their external experience. External conditions, no matter how seemingly or essentially negative, will adapt themselves to our consciousness.

The mind is cause to all else. Once we understand that there is an inevitable harmony between our thinking and our lives, we can bring all the good things we want into our existence. It is a long, cumulative process, but it is an immutable law of the universe.

AFFIRMATION

There is a harmony in the universe that makes it possible for me to create the life I want.

My life is my own creation. The anger and meanness that exist in the world around me need not become a part of my inner life. I have the power to draw to myself what is good.

I rejoice in my ability to create a beautiful life in the image of my thought with all the power of the universe to make it so.

ME in YOU

The silence
I said was yours
grew from within.

The anger
that lived in your heart
lay in mine.

The fears
drawn from your gut
filled my stomach, my heart, my
life.

Your weakness
in my limbs
kept me from walking away.

I played the fool
it seemed your fool
until I found
it was me.

3 Comfort

Comfort may be the most precious gift we have to give each other. Just as being comforted helps us develop healthy and resilient spirits, the lack of comfort in time of need, especially in childhood, weakens our ability to live well. Once we learn to heal the part of us that never received the support we needed as a child, we can fill our lives with the simple and beautiful joys of being a comfort to each other.

Our greatest memories of comfort usually come from early in life. Most of us remember moments of special tenderness—being held, read to, put to bed with a kiss and a hug. We recall special cookies and treats, tears being wiped away, wounds healed. Even more important were moments when our problems were understood, our faults forgiven, our efforts appreciated. Likewise, some of our greatest hurts are times when such comfort and tenderness were absent. Such care is a central part of growing up as a strong, confident, and loving adult and remains with us, both as a precious memory and as inner strength.

Yet no matter what our life experience, we can all be comforted. We can take action to strengthen our ability to love and be loved in our adult lives. Using a technique called creative visualization, you can call to mind a situation which was hurtful to you as a child and create a happy and satisfying ending in your mind. Our consciousness will respond to such vision and will feel a partial healing of the hurt. The more often the process is repeated, the greater the healing.

Many will find this implausible, questioning the ability of the mind to heal itself. They doubt that feeling the pain involved in rethinking past hurts can do us any good. Yet there are countless people who have learned to heal their hearts. And once we make the effort to clear our consciousness of childhood hurts, experience will show us that the process of inner healing can greatly enrich our lives.

Visualize a situation from your childhood where comfort was needed but not given. Recall the hurt of that moment... Now imagine a parent, a loving adult or even a friend coming to your aid. Allow yourself to feel how you would have felt had this happened... Enjoy it, appreciate it, savor it... You are loved, cared for and comforted because you deserve all the loving support you need... You will feel a change in your deepest self. In a small way, step by step, you are being healed.

It is not easy to deal with the hurts that remain in our hearts. Yet our desire to enter into loving relationships and our satisfaction as we experience the healing of our hurts give us the courage to look within. We long to both give and receive the care we all need. As we heal our own hurts, we grow in stature and naturally learn to be a comfort to each other.

AFFIRMATION

I live in a universe that will always comfort me in time of need. I have only to open myself to the healing forces in and around me.

Within my being lies the power to heal all my hurts. I reach through my inner self, visualizing the under-standing and comfort I need to live life well. I also reach to the world around me, opening myself to the beauty, harmony and love that are comforting to my spirit. The goodness of life heals my spirit and gives me the strength to be a comfort to myself and to others.

Comfort

Take me back to a time when
sweet parent-talk
harbored hope and
laughter praised life,

when hurts were heard
humming, then lifted
liltingly, lovingly
through the air.

Take me back to a place where
fears softened in flight
and slowly seeped
out into winter winds,

where anger melted like
icicles held by
noonday suns and
quickening body heat,

when tears of struggle were
kissed with kindness
and effort turned to strength
sheltered in soothing sounds.

4 The Use of Meditation

The essence of meditation is to touch the divinity of our innermost being. It is a conscious effort to bring regularly into our lives the beauty, comfort and joy that we have all experienced in fleeting glimpses. Based on the belief that the divine lies in all of us, meditation is a form of prayer that makes use of both mind and body to connect in a deeper way with that power we call God.

Those of us who have been raised in Western religious tradition have been taught that connecting with the divine is primarily an interaction between our inner selves and a personal God, who can be angry or pleased, helpful or resistant to our desires. Meditation, on the other hand, involves a process of opening ourselves to an impersonal divine power within. Many believe this represents a rejection of God and of sincere spirituality.

But both meditation and traditional religious practices serve to help the individual find spiritual fulfillment. In fact, numerous religious writers, such as Anthony de Mello, S.J. have explained how to interweave these two methods of finding God. In *Sadhana, A Way to God*, Father de Mello describes Christian exercises in Eastern form. He explains that his goal is simply to use meditation to help people pray. We need not be afraid to broaden our spiritual approach.

Meditation begins with emptying our minds of worldly thoughts and feelings, creating a silence within us. There are countless techniques of freeing the mind of its mundane distractions, but their general focus is to center the mind on the physical functioning of the body, especially on our breathing. Feeling the flow of life's blood through our bodies and noting the sensations of individual parts of the body are also important in creating the inner quiet which allows an opening to the divine.

However, our ability to achieve a meditative state is based on more than use of such techniques. Another important factor is maintaining a healthy body, keeping ourselves free of artificial stimulants and depressants, getting sufficient exercise and rest, and consuming a healthy diet of natural foods. The closer our bodies are to being as nature intended, the easier it is for us to connect with our inner selves.

Meditation is one way we can bring God into our lives. Body and mind interact to reach spiritual truth, which is that we are enveloped by the love and beauty of the universe. We are meant to be one with the harmony and peace of realities greater than ourselves. We are meant to join ourselves with the divine.

AFFIRMATION

*Human understanding has the
power to reach beyond our
ordinary thoughts and emotions.
Truth and harmony lie at the
heart of all of us.*

*I move along a path of discovery,
taking time each day to quiet my
worldly distractions and connect
with the divine goodness that is
part of my being.*

*I hold to my heart all the comfort
and understanding that arise
from an ever-increasing oneness
with the eternal qualities of truth
and unending love.*

Life's Breath

Breathing in and down
through
my deepest self,

flowing into the warm embrace
of what was meant to be,

carried by my breath into
the harmony that is all.

5 Mistakes

One of the most painful aspects of human existence is facing our mistakes. Yet the alternative is to persist in harming ourselves and others. We have within us the honesty, intelligence, and courage to take responsibility for our lives and to overcome our errors.

Every mind has protective mechanisms which make it easy for us to avoid confronting ourselves and dealing with our mistakes. Take, for example, people who constantly find fault with others. Why do they persist in such harmful behavior? Because they really don't see what they are doing. It would be too painful. Something in them urges them to behave that way, and as long as they are blind to the harm they are causing, there is no incentive to face a painful problem.

Judgmental people are not alone. We all have faults and make mistakes. Yet our minds go to great lengths to protect us from the truth of our errors. This is easy to understand if you take a minute to think of something you have done that was a mistake... Did you think of something very minor or something that wasn't really a mistake? If so, you are protecting yourself by avoiding the issue. When we think of something that was genuinely hurtful to ourselves or to others, we feel pain. And if we do not perceive a way to resolve that issue, to repair the damage, to change ourselves, we will move away from that pain by refusing to deal with the problem.

The key to finding the courage to be honest with ourselves about our faults lies in understanding that we are fundamentally good and strong beings. Our innermost selves are neither sullied by error nor incapable of change. We are part of a universe that allows us to be whatever we want to be. Any mistake can be forgiven. Any hurt we have caused can be healed. The path to dealing effectively and courageously with our faults begins with seeing the truth about ourselves and taking one step at a time to constructive living.

It is part of the human condition to err. That does not separate us from the power to do the right thing and to act in ways that are in the best interest of everyone. We can correct our mistakes, heal the hurts they have caused, and build a consciousness where good judgment grows and becomes a natural part of our existence.

AFFIRMATION

*There is a universe in and
around me that forgives my
mistakes, gathers me into its life,
and joins me with the right
thinking that is mine.*

*I recognize that all my
decisions will not be the best
ones. Yet mistakes do not
destroy the goodness that is
natural to my being.
Acknowledging my errors, I
work through them and learn
to see beyond what limits my
thought.*

*Reaching for my intuitive
knowledge of right action, I rise
above my mistakes and
allow myself to be an imperfect
creature striving for union with
the truth and goodness in and
around me.*

Moving Mountains

Mistakes fill mountains
around every man's plain
higher than the sight
of stubborn-straight
level gaze

Until the eye fills
at its massive plight
all around, at every turn
what fault has built
as barrier to the world.

Then mountains can move
or seem smaller in time
as life grows within
reaching over and through
what can no longer contain
vision larger than itself.

6 Dreams

Have you considered lately what you want in life? Most people's first reaction to this question is to bypass the true issue with superficial answers like to "get rich," to "be successful," or to "stay young forever." But what is really being asked goes much deeper. Only when we understand our innermost selves and the needs and desires that motivate our actions, can we fully comprehend what will bring us the satisfaction of living well.

We all know instinctively that there are longings that come from deep within ourselves. Some of us feel the need to develop a talent like music or mathematics. Others take great pleasure in creating something that is beautiful or a product that functions effectively. When we discover our own unique variety of talents and desires, we are in a position to find and enjoy the good we want in our lives.

Think back to the relatively uncluttered world of your childhood when outside demands intruded so much less in your mental life. What inner stirrings existed for you? Think back to an activity that brought joy, that you sense came not from sharing with a loved person or from praise earned from others. What was one thing that you naturally did when left alone that filled you with pleasure and satisfaction? Imagine how you felt when you were acting out those desires. Then you will rediscover an essential part of your being. You will see a direction in which you can find what you are seeking.

Why are such feelings so important to recognize and fulfill? Because it is our nature to do so. They come from within, from our connection with a universal power, rather than from our environment. Of course, they may be encouraged or discouraged from the outside. A parent's interest in woodwork could help a child develop a desire he already has to build something beautiful. But it is the child's intrinsic desire that leads to fulfillment.

Once we discover the longings that are primary to our being and once we understand that our deepest desires are part of a greater whole, we will naturally move toward making our dreams come true. We can recapture and develop the joy and satisfaction we knew earlier in life. We can become one with universal right action. This is the way to "get rich," "be successful," and "stay young forever."

AFFIRMATION

*I am part of a greater conscious-
ness that draws me toward a full
life. Thus arise my interests, my
desires, my dreams. These are
my most precious possessions
because they show me the path
to my greater good.*

*I take the time to look within to
the source of my longings. In
my innermost being I find an
understanding of the needs
and desires I must fulfill to live
life well.*

*Knowing that my deepest
desires are finite parts of the
Infinite Whole, I realize that they,
too, are right and good and that
all nature and life converge to
help me make my dreams
come true*

Dreams

Did you ever wish you were young
and want to dream dreams
so real
they would take your breath away?

I myself wish I had a heart
so safe
its dreams would go on smiling
breathing life to my life
no matter how old I might grow.

Yet I know there are dreams
for the young and the old
that draw willing minds
to reach to the soul
and bring our lives to them.

Longings of the Soul

There is a correspondence between the natural world around us and the inner selves we seek to know. Understanding this bond provides us an opening to the deepest realities of our existence. Through our connection with nature we can reach into our being and be one with the longings that enrich our lives. Hidden realities of our being become clear. Nature becomes the gateway to the soul.

First we must observe and appreciate how the world around us mirrors our own nature. There are countless examples of the ways our deepest longings are reflected in the natural universe. Our need for peace is seen in the purring cat, lying in the sunshine, tummy in the air, not a care in the world. The courage of the human spirit is mirrored in new growth fighting for life after the devastation of fire. Our love of play corresponds to the chasing squirrels, leaping from branch to branch.

Yet an intellectual appreciation of such correspondence is only the beginning of self-understanding and growth. We must open our hearts, that is, allow ourselves to feel the peace of the purring cat, the joy of animals at play, the courage and energy of new life. Thus we draw upon and enlarge potential that lies in our deepest selves.

Once this opening of the self is begun, we can take a further step to reach to the soul. By simply quieting the mind and observing in calm the world around us, new truths about our own nature are revealed. A silent wood can become alive with sentiment drawn from the inner self. For each of us nature's gift of understanding differs, a surprise, a unique expression of the divine life within us.

All nature has the power to evoke in us the highest qualities of our inner selves, grounded in universal truth. Observing birds in flight might give rise to a sense of grace, joy, purposefulness or freedom. Whatever our response, it is uniquely our own. To the extent that we are willing to stop and think about how such things make us feel, we learn truths we might never perceive without them. Thus we draw on our capacity to bring into our conscious experience our deepest longings.

We all have a sense of the longings of the soul. Yet that inner reality so often remains closed off to our conscious experience. We can choose to reach to the natural world around us to enlarge our experience. We can learn from the responses that arise from deep within our being. We can let nature draw our minds and hearts to a new harmony with the longings of the soul.

AFFIRMATION

My inner self is part of a universal whole. As I respond to the divinity in the natural world around me, I open to my experience the corresponding good that lies in my soul.

My deepest longings are toward what will enrich my being. The good in me longs to be part of my conscious life and a closeness with nature provides an opening to these inner realities of the soul.

I believe in the oneness of mind, spirit and the world around me. In opening my spirit to the natural union of all life, I find peace.

Longings of the Soul

Kinder spirits
would follow the raindrops
seeking their source
and find strength
to live in peace

More gentle beings
would flow with each night sound
riding wave after wave
of life-filled delight
and fill all their needs

But some long most deeply
to soar above treetops
to feel all the force
all the fire of life
burning deep in the soul.

The Need for Love and Fear

A life well lived is based on a healthy balance between love and fear. The nourishing power of love energizes our lives and the protective power of fear leads us away from harm. While excessive fear can be debilitating, both love and fear help us create the sense of well-being we seek in our lives.

Love is the force which embraces. It draws us toward what is beautiful. Love of learning, of accomplishment, of our fellow beings—all keep us moving in a direction that makes life worthwhile. Loving is felt as excitement, determination and satisfaction. It causes us to draw on what is best in ourselves. This is why we long to have love in our lives.

On the other hand, a complete attitude of love would open the individual to all experience and invite disaster. What if we had no fear of burning stoves or of mean-spirited people? What if we welcomed our own character flaws? We need more than the attraction of loving, positive forces to make good choices and to take responsibility for our lives.

Fear is the energy which closes off what we perceive as dangerous. Both children and adults learn to control behavior from a combination of love and fear. Children say thank you and study for tests. Adults work long hours and do not drink and drive. Fear is uncomfortable and sometimes painful, but it can lead us to a better self.

While fear can be helpful, too much of it can cripple our ability to move ahead. Yet many people find themselves more drawn to fearfulness than to a positive attitude. Tell someone you expect the economy to decline and a sympathetic response will almost surely come. Say the opposite and you will likely encounter hostility.

This is true because positive and loving energies challenge the individual. They essentially represent openness, commitment, achievement. Negativity indicates that what is needed is inaction. It feels safe to withdraw because only when we try can we fail.

In seeking the best for ourselves, we first turn to the energizing force of love. And we avoid a fearfulness which paralyzes us. But we also need to keep in mind that love and fear are both necessary to a life well lived.

AFFIRMATION

I am naturally drawn to the beauty, accomplishment and satisfaction I desire. The inspiration I need to live life well lies within.

Recognizing both the positive energies of love and the protective aspects of fear, I open myself to the hopes and desires that lead me to all I can be.

I have the power to direct my own path, to protect myself from harm, to move toward my own well-being. And there I find peace.

Heart's Hope

Sparks of self ignite
what has long lain
waiting
snatches of mind-thought,
dreams, heart's hope
for the beautiful
unashamedly enflamed
to reach to soul's end
peaceful private glow.

Love warms and curls the
edges of my sleep
lest I fall
into others' fears
finding my heart's longing.

9 Learning to Change

Everyone wants to change something. There is always some aspect of our lives that is unsatisfactory, some way that we sense a need to repair what is hurt or to grow beyond our present reality. And indeed, change is always taking place, whether we seek it or not. The issue is whether or not we are willing to make the effort necessary to control that change.

The rock opera "Tommy" expresses what most people want from change: "See me, feel me, touch me, heal me." We long to be changed through the love and comfort of an outside power. In this way we bypass the need to understand the nature of our problems and to take the responsibility for dealing with them. It is natural to hope that solutions to our problems will arise from beyond the selves that are in trouble rather than from that source of truth within all of us.

Yet, this behavior leaves us as children at the mercy of the known or unknown powers that might choose to satisfy our needs and desires. Empowerment lies in the knowledge that changes in ourselves can be understood and largely controlled. We can become aware of the forces that cause change and learn how these forces can be used to create the kind of changes we want in our lives.

The way we think is deeply affected by the experiences that our minds process. What we choose to read, from inspirational literature to mystery novels, what we consistently hear, from formal lectures to gossip, the movies and television we choose to see, uplifting or depressing, all represent new information that changes what we are, how we think, how we feel. We can control a great deal of what we make a part of our thinking.

Not only can we control what we put into our minds, we can alter the way we process such outside experience. Every idea, act or sensation becomes what it means to us through an interaction of the outside input and the nature of our consciousness. As we make the effort to reach for the positive in our lives, we gradually build an inner life that sees our experience in the best possible light and responds naturally to what enriches our being. We can also use meditation and affirmations to develop a consciousness that leads us to constructive living.

We can largely control both what we choose to take into our minds and hearts and the inner reality that interacts with outside experience. The strength and resilience of our consciousness grows with our concerted efforts to bring into our thinking what supports our growth and well-being. We can all live lives of our own creation.

AFFIRMATION

The universe is designed for change and life is filled with energy and vitality that overcome all impediment.

As part of this universal whole, I feel the power within me to create the beautiful and fulfilling life I desire. I take charge of my life, turning toward experience that frees and enriches my being.

I own my own self and rejoice in every simple step that brings me to the satisfying life I desire.

Land of my Own Creation

I cry for myself, for my safe arrival
in a land of my own creation,
where satisfaction needs no echo
and joy is its own stimulation.

I celebrate the death of hungry need
and a new life of calming passion
for what frees and fulfills
longings that feed the heart.

I salute every simple step
thousands and thousands of moves
from homelessness to enfoldment
in loving arms of my own creation.

10 The Power of the Universe

Humankind knows that there is a principle whereby solutions to problems appear. Issues are resolved when we open ourselves to the power of the universe—God, Universal Mind—whatever we might call such a force. The great religions of the world acknowledge this truth and encourage their members to give up the struggles of problem-solving to a higher power.

The reason for this general agreement is that we can all see the outward manifestation of this power or principle. Practically everyone has experienced feeling confused, frightened and unable to deal with a situation, turning to a higher power for a solution, and successfully resolving the issue. This is the essence of prayer in all religions. Not only does the way we deal with outward reality change, but so does the inner self. We experience peace and harmony when we create that channel of openness to spiritual power.

Other ways of relating to this higher power have been proposed through time. In the nineteenth century, Ralph Waldo Emerson proposed that humanity could best relate to God through interaction with nature and by connecting with the spiritual quality in our deepest selves. The Emersonian concept is that we all have access to the divine spirit that exists in the nature of all life.

What is most important is to open our hearts, to reach to the beauty and peace in and around us with serenity. This power is intrinsic in us and in the natural world around us. It will work its principles in and of itself. In order to connect with universal good, we work to create a peaceful and receptive mind which believes in our inner ability to know what is right and to create good in our lives.

The ability to open ourselves to the power for good in the universe is in our grasp. It is something we can learn to do, practice and increasingly use in an effective manner. Practical results encourage us. Gradually our ability to begin each day with a closeness to the universe deepens as a God-consciousness recreates our lives.

Using the power of the universe is a principle which works. The more we give to its discovery and practical application, the greater our ability to control our lives. The power to heal the body and the spirit is held in our minds and in our hearts. It is up to us to make it happen.

AFFIRMATION

My mind is a unique part of the divinity of the universe. It holds unlimited power to bring good into my life.

I know that that I can heal my hurts and create the existence I desire. I make the effort to connect with the healing power within.

It is my nature to live in harmony with the goodness of the universe. I choose to open myself to the divinity in and around me. I am one with the natural healing quality of all life.

Setting my Heart Free

I take back my heart
and set it free
in a comfortable place
where sun pours lightly
into quiet morning sounds

Where steamy rain smells
sift through doors
open to life
and pleasures grow from one another
like daffodils in fertile ground

And where a cooling, light caress
reaches through evening
to hold through the night
all of its creatures
who have ever longed to sing.

Anger

Anger can be a healthy response to what is damaging to our wellbeing. It is a natural reaction that energizes us and promotes change, leading to a return to harmony in our lives. But anger is incompatible with loving feelings and must be acted upon and released, restoring the peaceful consciousness we all seek.

When something hurtful or harmful to the individual occurs, a healthy spirit will feel a sense of anger. Being physically or mentally harmed should arouse a response in us that leads to our putting a stop to the offense. In simple cases, someone closes a door on your finger, you cry in dismay, they profusely apologize, you get over it.

Unfortunately, unhealthy responses to being hurt can become a serious problem. It can happen that whoever hurt you might not be sorry. They might fail to feel a normal apologetic response. They might even be glad they hurt you, for whatever reasons. It is also possible that what causes you harm might be impersonal, an act of nature, which rarely expresses regret. The point is that when we feel anger, we often do not get responses that would help us heal.

On the other hand, it could be that when our sense of well-being is violated, we ourselves might be unable to feel a healthy response. Someone could take advantage of us and we could feel glad to have helped them get what they want. We could get yelled at and turn away, succeeding in feeling nothing. At least, it might seem that way. But harm will result from blocking an appropriately angry response.

It is important to set our minds straight about how we respond to what harms us. We need to acknowledge our anger where it is appropriate and to express it in a healthy way. Then it is up to us to actively seek the love and comfort that will further dissolve the anger we feel. Friends who express support and compassion can help us regain a sense of balance. Quiet times in peaceful, natural settings, curling up under warm covers with a book, doing anything we love to do, is healing. Such positive experiences are all the more effective as we consciously direct them toward the healing of our pain.

There is no hurt too great to be healed, no heart too angry to be restored to its natural resiliency and sense of order. We have the power to deal with situations that cause anger in a healthy way. We can connect with the harmony and peace at the center of our being.

AFFIRMATION

*The universe surrounds me with
what I need to deal with anger,
heal hurts and find peace in
my life.*

*I recognize that anger directs me
to my own good. It energizes
me to move away from harm. I
release anger as it serves its
purpose and fills no further need
in my life.*

*The world is a natural environ-
ment for my healing. I use anger
well and release it freely,
returning to the peaceful
consciousness it is my nature
to seek.*

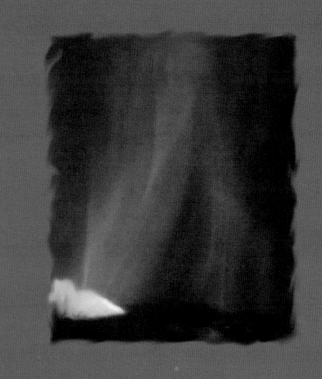

44

Healing Our Hearts

Let day begin
with a curve
of the back
lifted to life

Speckled light
dancing
on pillow softness

Tangled hair
tickling lightly
while toes
curl
in anticipation
of the new day

As radiator warmth
blends with bed-body heat
to soften anger's icy hold.

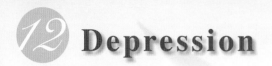

12 Depression

The most violent enemy of the contentment, peace and joy that make life worthwhile is depression. Anger turned inward ravages the center of affections we call the heart. Only with release of our anger and the comfort of loving support can inner balance and love of life be restored.

Almost everyone has experienced some form of depression in the sense of feeling "down," discouraged about our ability to find happiness in life. But we realize that some ups and downs, some sadness and disappointment are a necessary part of life. It is the debilitating effect of chronic depression that destroys our ability to live well, primarily because of our sense of helplessness in controlling our inner lives.

Psychology teaches that depression can be combatted through the use of drugs, electro-shock therapy or by dealing with the anger we have turned toward ourselves. The difficulties involved in releasing anger and healing our hearts are often so great that many give up the hope of restoring the natural harmonies of a healthy life. They simply try to alter the body's chemistry to achieve a balanced state of mind and spirit.

Since depression often represents our anger at past hurts, the kind of healing we need to deal with it involves a revisiting of these hurtful experiences. We need a healthy release of the anger and the feeling that we are forgiven for our mistakes. We need to believe that our inner beings are cherished by whatever is good in the universe. All of this represents a tremendous challenge.

One reason why depression is so hard to deal with is that it is rooted in the feeling that the fault lies in ourselves. Why did we allow this to happen to us? Why were we unable to defend ourselves against so much hurt? And why can we not lift ourselves from the weight that overwhelms us from within? Criticism is painful to everyone, but when someone else finds fault with us, we tend to put most of the blame on their error. When we are our own accuser, as in depression, there seems no escape from our pain.

The most effective thing we can do to deal with depression is to take one step in the right direction. We know we must release the anger. There are books, doctors, friends, spiritual resources which can help us. There are sources of positive energy, like fresh air and exercise, which give us strength to deal with our pain. We must, above all, believe that the simplest beginning in dealing with the problem is the beginning of our hope. There is laughter and love around us. Let us believe that it can be ours tomorrow.

AFFIRMATION

*The universe holds me in its
arms, listens to my hurts and
heals my heart. I have only to
open myself to the truth of the
divine goodness in and
around me.*

*Whatever has hurt me is part of
my past. I have the power to be
free from anything that threatens
my happiness today. I have the
power to believe in a
better tomorrow.*

*All good and right thinking is
given freely. I let it heal my
heart, one day at a time, and
restore the hope that is a natural
part of all life.*

Faith in the Night

Let us remember
laughter that
runs in rivulets
like a tear

Love that
shines through
darkness
like a smile

And faith that
kisses
filled with tenderness
will touch us
in the night.

13 The Richness of Life

There are times when all of us question our ability to enjoy the depth of feeling, fulfillment and richness of the life we desire. That is why generations of students have been deeply moved by T. S. Eliot's conclusion that he does not think the mermaids "will sing to me." But the mermaids are always there for us. In fact, the joy and feeling the mermaids represent can never be taken away because they arise from our innermost selves.

Most children are actively engaged in a world they perceive to be made for their pleasure. They expect that parents should love them enormously. Friends and teachers should fill each day with interest and fun. And young people rarely forget how to feel. They are openly disappointed if there isn't plenty of ice cream, distressed at the ending of each day. Only the saddest of children fear that birds, mermaids or all of life might prefer to sing for someone who could respond more deeply.

But as time passes, life creates doubts in the confident expectations of childhood. It becomes apparent that loving support from parents is not always forthcoming, that friends and teachers can be hurtful, and that we can stop feeling the hopefulness of each new day. We all feel confusion about such disappointments. Does the world deny us the sense of well-being we want most in life, or are we not capable or worthy of receiving what we need?

If we come to the conclusion that life holds no joy for us to receive, we are overlooking a great deal. Certainly, the pleasures children know arise from experience which is available to all of us. The kinds of things that brought satisfaction in the past are there for us now. We have only to reach for them. While life presents many challenges and cannot be lived without pain, there is, at the same time, endless opportunity for fulfillment.

As we open ourselves to the feelings that are natural to our being, life will respond to our desire. Being closed off from life is a temporary sensation. And rather than a lack of feeling, it is a very deep feeling that can be altered, a capacity that can be used more positively. Human beings have the potential for happiness and satisfaction. Morning song is for everyone. Kindness and compassion reach to all humankind. There are no dead souls.

We must never lose sight of the potential in us for the satisfaction we desire in life. Our inner selves long to feel the richness of the world around us. We know this is true because we all remember when not only the birds, but all life, seemed to be singing especially for us.

AFFIRMATION

The enriching life of the universe is my life. The world around me is poised to respond to my inner self.

I feel the warmth of sunshine, the soothing power of rain, the sweetness of birdsong. They comfort my deepest self. In the same way, I open myself to all that brings me what I desire.

I fill my life with the good that is mine. My innermost being echoes the richness of life.

Sing to Me

Morning mists rise
and reach to me
to soften the tangles
that harden my life
to unfold the worries
binding my heart.

Birds, singing each to each,
sing to me, too,
help loosen the ties
unravel the cares
releasing bound hopes
to fly with them, free.

$\mathcal{14}$ **Longings of Love**

Love is the pleasure of drawing to ourselves and becoming one with what attracts us. When we take in the feeling of a beautiful day, we respond to the sunshine, not to the heavy traffic. We make this choice when our inner selves are drawn more to joy than to stress. The sunshine is what we love. In the same way, when we love others, we are drawn to a part of them that responds to our innermost selves. It might be kindness we sense in them, or it might be their ability to dominate us. In either case, we long to become one with what strikes a responsive chord in our hearts.

The feeling of love causes us to draw to ourselves what love desires. Take, for example, a love for plant life. This not only brings us pleasure as we watch ferns green and flowers bloom. It also leads us to go outside and "work" in the yard and do all kinds of things related to this affection. It draws to us others who have the same interest and pleasure. Our loves bring into our lives what reflects longings that arise from our innermost being.

In the same way, we can be attracted to what is destructive to our well-being. Think of some type of negative situation that keeps recurring in your life. Painful as it may be, in some way you are drawn to that. It is not just bad luck which causes us to repeat hurtful experiences. We harbor a love for some aspect of what is happening there. When our own consciousness is filled with pain, we feel somehow satisfied or justified in drawing to ourselves the part of the world which reflects that same view of life.

Such behavior is clearly a distortion of the perception of good. The root of the problem lies in an inner picture of ourselves as unworthy. We reach out to the world to take in what feels comfortable to that false sense of self. It is easy to lose sight of our divine nature as we struggle with the problems of life. We take in our failures and disappointments, often forgetting or rejecting the successes and personal growth arising from them, because the negative feels comfortable in a heart that fails to rejoice in itself.

We can restore to our consciousness the true concept of our divine nature. Once we feel the good in ourselves, we will naturally respond and draw to ourselves the boundless good in the world around us.

AFFIRMATION

*The universe brings to me the
longings of my heart. What I
love will naturally and easily
come into my life.*

*I appreciate and nurture the
good in me and I draw on the
divinity that flows through me to
fill my being with the love that
enriches my life. In the same
way, I clear out the negativity in
my consciousness, having no
desire to draw to myself what is
destructive.*

*The power of the universe
responds to my effort to be one
with the divinity within me. My
world is filled with the loving
harmony I desire.*

Music in Me

There is music in me now,
that outside chorus
echoes, expands, sings

From the second I turned
to hear the same song
that reached from my being

When evening's saving sound
led me to turn in the cool air
to draw to myself the harmony
irresistible to my heart

When all life joined in the
symphony it longed to be.

15 Passion

There are hungers of mankind that long to be satisfied by the rich healing qualities of romantic love. The magnetism of such longings between two beings can be among life's most thrilling and satisfying experiences. Yet passion, while capable of healing hurts and comforting man's intrinsic loneliness, is also more than likely to cause devastation along with joy. Our only hope for behaving wisely in these matters is to direct the development of our inner selves over a long period of time, fostering a healthy consciousness that longs for its own good.

Passionate love involves a powerful attraction, unparalleled happiness, and an excitement that goes to the core of our being. Not only does the beloved appear in the best possible light, we do also, and indeed the whole world puts its best foot forward. Rainfall becomes a cooling refreshment, while the sun warms us to the core of our being, creating a zest for all aspects of life. Being in love makes us feel good, valuable, worthy of esteem. It is safety from disappointment and failure. It is a world unto itself.

Naturally all right-thinking people would want to stay "in love" all the time, if it were not for the side effects. Insecurity, jealousy, fear of loss—all hover in the background. There are many sources of such feelings. Doubts may arise from instinctive warnings that the object of our passion may not be worthy of our devotion. Or we may simply not fully trust what was given so inexplicably. Life experience teaches that passion is not durable. The joy of passion is mitigated by lucid moments which reveal the imperfections and complications of real life.

The other fundamental problem with what can be among the most beautiful of life experiences is that we often long to fill every need, every hope, every weakness with such passion. We seek our power outside ourselves—to heal our hurts, to make us the beautiful beings we aspire to be. Unfortunately, in the process, we can lose the very selves we seek to perfect. We become enslaved, prisoners to the desire to please or to fill the desires of the beloved. Yet, this need not be the case.

Passionate love, like all longings, arises from the nature of our consciousness, and we can direct our passions by controlling what we ourselves are. Once we realize that falling in love is an urge to satisfy our inner selves, we have a new power over our lives. We can work to create a consciousness that attracts the positive and healthy qualities of our own spirit.

We are capable of being the kind of person who loves and is loved well, whose passions arise from a positive consciousness. We can learn to be the most loving of creatures who deserves only what mirrors the beauty of our own spirit.

AFFIRMATION

*The universe is filled with the
kind of love that enriches my life.
It is always ready to draw to me
the happiness and fulfillment
I desire.*

*I recognize my ability to be in
charge of my feelings. I am
not the victim of an unknown,
outside force that controls my
inner life, nor am I the victim
of passionate feelings that are
destructive to my good.*

*The loves of my life mirror the
strength of my inner self. I am a
loving being who deserves the
fulfillment of my deepest desires
for good.*

Heart's Longing

From deep within the warmth
of shared comfort and joy
we heard our heart's longing-

"I was once so alone,"
we said, just as one,
and our hearts moved to sing

As the rich sounds of life
of music and our laughter
healed what was hurt

And the strains of our symphony
filled every part of that world
where violin passion feeds life.

16 Promises of Marriage

From the first whispered tenderness to the moral and legal commitment of vows, marriage is full of promises. Our minds and hearts are full of pledges that often remain unspoken, in some cases buried so deep within ourselves that we scarcely realize they exist. Being clear about the kinds of promises we are making and our ability to keep them is the first step to a successful marriage.

Some hidden promises can cause the marriage to self-destruct unless we are courageous enough to give them a closer look. What if someone has the silent intention to heal the emotional hurts of their partner? What if someone intends to hold their pain within themselves to keep the marriage on an even keel? We need to let all our promises into the light of day to make sure this is what both parties really want.

There are also the promises we make out loud. I will love you no matter what the future holds. I will put your needs before my own. I will always be there for you. It is amazing that we believe we can do these things as we say them! Besides that problem, there is the issue of keeping promises like this. We may feel that it would be desirable to love someone no matter what, but can we realistically make that kind of promise?

The best promise we can make to one another is to try to accept the responsibilities involved in growing side by side. Unfortunately, that does not have a romantic ring to it! But the shocking truth is that loving our partner begins with loving ourselves. We need to grow spiritually and emotionally. This empowers us to be a loving and supportive partner.

While longings for intimacy, passion and security are at the heart of romance, we need to be clear about how to make this happen. Only by being self-aware and courageous about dealing with our personal issues can we be a great marriage partner, seeing the good in our partner, being supportive, giving them space to grow.

We cannot promise to make life safe for another person and we cannot expect another to do that for us. We are each responsible for what we become. But we can commit to being the best person we can be, starting by loving and accepting ourselves. Then we can share this wonderful energy with our partner. This is how we love one another as we love ourselves.

AFFIRMATION

Life's longing for love and marriage leads me to a better self. It energizes my being and makes it possible for me to meet the challenges of a shared life.

The promises of marriage begin with me. I will nurture myself so that my energy is a gift to my partner. I will cherish the growth of another as I do my own.

The love I have enriches my life because it is in loving that I grow to be the person of my dreams.

The Sweetness of Care

Beginning in gentleness
far greater than I have known,
a lightness stirs and
moves to fill quiet spaces
*   between us*

Disparities traversed with
tenderness and with child-hope
that lightens the step
and gives it joy, like a dancer
*   in flight*

And the sweetness of care
grows back and forth in waves
that reach further and further
for long, longing moments
*   within us.*

Father Love

The importance of a father's love is understood more than ever today as "We get pregnant" and Dad gets maternity leave. Each parent makes a unique contribution to raising their children. There is a natural role, there are special gifts, that only a father can bring to his child.

Many would say that this is typecasting, that there are no real differences between what a dad and a mom have to offer. Look at the issue of discipline. Traditionalists would say this is primarily the role of the dad. Likewise for supporting the family financially and keeping the house structurally sound. The not-for-dad list includes such things as dusting the furniture and making ballet buns for their daughters. But we all know that today there is great interchange between parents in their roles in child rearing. Most moms have jobs outside the home and some dads have been known to dust!

But even though parents often change traditional roles, in spite of the fact that each one can do most of what is traditionally expected of the other, there is a special love that can only come from a father. Those of us who have been single moms understand this as no one else can. We have sensed the need for pure masculinity in a role model for our sons and as a joy to our daughters. We have sought out uncles and friends to provide this for our children. We have appreciated male teachers and coaches who helped fill this need. But it is never the same.

It is not necessary to attempt a complete list. What is important is to understand that connections between parents and children arise from a very deep, instinctual place and that each gender has something special to share with the children.

We give all we can to our children. If our role is that of a single parent, we attempt to provide everything our children need. We try to be moms and dads all in one. But in the connection between hearts, we can only give what we have. A father's love arises from a special place where only a guy can be. All children, from time to time, need to reach there.

AFFIRMATION

We live in a world filled with parent-love. The special bond between father and child is precious beyond belief. I will always appreciate that.

I will be everything I can for my children, reaching to the depths of my being to give them what they need.

The rewards of parenting are mine because I have given my heart and opened my deepest self to the children I love.

Dad

In my dreams
it was all perfect
only me
filled with care
and pride

No time for loss
or disappointment

Always time
for me.

18 Mother Love

It is natural for mothers to love with a depth and passion that exceed life itself, and every child longs to be the recipient of such immense and enriching care. Yet the complexities of life interfere with our giving and receiving the nurture of mother love.

For both boys and girls, there are needs that only a father can meet. However, there is a sense that a mother's love is even more essential to a child's emotional well-being. We believe mother love to be so deep and unquestioning that no matter what the sin, no matter how great the failure, a mother will see what is good in her child. Experience shows us that this expectation is often justified, especially in times of great disappointment and pain.

The unique bond between mother and child begins, of course, in the womb. Under the best circumstances, the love between marriage partners is extended and enriched by the existence of this incarnation of their passion. As the child grows from the nurture of her own body, mothers feel the harmony of their existence together, for a time as one. Then the pain of childbirth adds an intensity to the love, as so much is given so that another might live. Thus it should be, and so on through the child's life, in the best of all possible worlds.

But life is not so easy, and intensity of feeling can easily go awry as diverse pressures weaken our ability to be all our children need. Indeed, a parent's feeling for her child can even become destructive to them both. Sometimes mothers turn to children for the fulfillment they lack in their own lives. Sometimes a child's needs can become impossible to meet. There are, unfortunately, too many cases where mother love turns to manipulation, disappointment or rage.

We all feel that our mothers should love us, understand us and be supportive of our endeavors. And we believe that they should forgive us our faults. Mothers should rise above any difficulty, overcome any obstacle to be the center of a loving family life that is so dear to us. But mothers are human.

There is no other being in the world who has a stronger bond with us than a mother who loves us more than life itself. Yet the closeness begun in the womb as a natural part of life is not so easily maintained. Let us recall the early harmonies and draw strength from them. Let us reach to what would have been easy and natural, had all life been good.

AFFIRMATION

*All nature cries for the
expression of love between
mother and child. The very
creation of life binds them.*

*I sense the loving bond with she
who gave me life. I recall the
harmonies of an earlier day and
the care that kept me safe. I hold
close to my being all the
tenderness of mother love.*

*The universe gives life and
heals all who love, but especially
mother and child who share
most deeply the communion of
all life.*

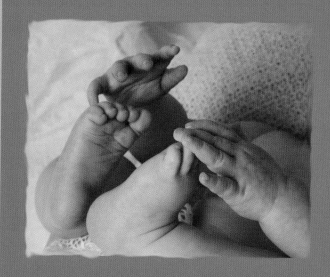

Mother Love

While peaceful plant life lives
and fills the air
slowly stirring
under softened lamp light,

She sings herself to sleep
with a gentle song,
special harmony
in tune with her needs.

And she slowly rocks the child
that sleeps already
comfortably at rest
in her heart of hearts,

As she feels a deep peace
alone with herself
and the child, mirrored
reflections of silent harmonies.

19 The Quality of Grace

The grace of ballerinas and of the most holy of souls lies at the heart of all of us. We are attracted to the physical and spiritual grace around us because it is in our nature to draw beauty to ourselves, to let it become a part of our being, joining our potential for grace and beauty more closely with the goodness of the universe.

Physical grace is most often associated with movement. There is an animal grace, as seen in dance, that embodies the lack of hindrance, the ease, and the dignity we seek in life. In the same way, the heart lifts to see ships glide on peaceful waters, part of the natural flow of sun and sea. We are transported by the lilt and fluidity of such effective and unimpeded movement. We feel the natural harmonies and beauty of a world that exudes the grace we seek in our lives.

Spiritual grace is most often associated with godliness or goodness. Certain people exude wisdom and loving kindness that seems to rise above the human condition. Such spiritual giants are venerated and their teachings taken up as models for the lives of others who long to draw this goodness into their own existence.

Yet both physical and spiritual grace manifest themselves in our lives every day. Think of actions in your own life that are filled with the sureness of a goal well set and the comfort that that goal can be easily achieved. Such acts need not be extraordinary ones. A mother taking a crying child into her arms is most graceful, as is a salesperson showing a product with a smile. Comfort, dignity, accomplishment – such qualities fill an action with grace and thus lend beauty to all of us as they are embodied in our lives.

In the same way, gracefulness of spirit arises from an understanding of what is true and good and from our efforts to bring those qualities more fully into our lives. Like the great religious leaders, we are all capable of joining with a higher power that informs us of the path to take and gives us the courage to proceed along that path. This is the essence of grace. As we possess it, that quality of goodness or godliness shines through our existence.

We, all of us, are the most beautiful of creatures in potential. Every time we act with accomplishment or reach within ourselves for the truth that lies in every heart, we are filled with grace. And day by day, the grace of such living becomes a larger part of our lives and glows from within.

AFFIRMATION

*I am drawn to the beauty of
the universe because it fulfills
longings in my deepest self. Any
bird's flight reflects the natural
movement of my spirit. I am one
with universal grace.*

*I move in comfort and
dignity through my day, feeling
the certainty that I know where
I am going and that I have the
innate ability to accomplish
my goals.*

*There is beauty, dignity and
strength all around me and in my
deepest soul. I long for it and
allow it to move me, with the
ease of the greening lawn,
toward what enriches my soul.*

Grace

My world will be sculpted
by hands filled with grace.

And life will arise
from moments of peace
moving freely,

Finite part of infinite whole
drawn from my part of life's mind.

20 Defying Defeat

The idea of defeat is so painful that is does emotional violence to the heart. Yet feelings of failure arise from a misunderstanding, both of the nature of the universe and of what has happened in our lives. We feel defeated when we have committed our hearts to someone or something, and all hope for a positive outcome seems lost. The truth is that experience is cyclical. The essential elements of any experience lie in others. There is always a chance to do better tomorrow.

We feel defeated when we have tried, and the extent of the heartfelt effort measures the extent of the pain of failure. Simply wanting something and not getting it is not defeat, but frustration. It causes anger and often curtails our energy, but remains on the periphery as a temporary setback. The essence of defeat is a sense of the irreparable and a feeling of personal responsibility for our failure.

Intellectually, we can deal with defeat through a clearer understanding of its true nature. Only those who have tried can feel defeat. It is for the worthy. Failure is also never totally our fault. In fact, it could be very largely the result of realities outside ourselves. And failure is never complete. We can always see some good in what we have undertaken. But the sense of defeat is also an emotion, and healing that hurt is primary to restoring the strength and confidence we need to move on.

The healing quality of laughter and tears is one of the mysteries of the soul. We know from experience that laughter brings us not only joy, but release and acceptance of a reality that is far from perfect. We laugh mostly at human foibles and in the laughter we forgive. Tears also nourish the soul and make it possible for us to accept that in some ways we have failed to measure up to the standards we have set for ourselves.

But what, above all, enables us to rise above our own weaknesses and disappointments is the good we find in ourselves. Failure was not total. There was much good in what we did and that good was motivated by love. And it is the love that lit our path that will give us the strength to believe in the essential goodness of our being and show us the way to move on to a better life.

Laughter, tears and love are the essence of our humanity, the grandeur of the human spirit. Here lies the power for good that overcomes obstacles and loves where there is fault. Only those who have not tried have never known failure. Only those who have never dreamed have never known defeat. We are human. Let us forgive our faults and open ourselves to a loving and fruitful tomorrow.

AFFIRMATION

I live in a healing universe.
My natural tendency is to be in
harmony with the divine order in
and around me.

I welcome the laughter that fills
my life and heals my soul. I
welcome the immense comfort
and release of heartfelt tears.
Both cleanse my soul and soften
my pain.

My spirit can never know defeat.
There is always enough love in
me to face my faults and enough
courage to see the way to
move on.

The Next Moment

Beginnings and ends
laughter and looking through tears
at what we leave behind
memories illumine the darkest heart.

The love that lit our path glows within
bringing light to the night
making possible the next moment
showing the way to move on.

21 Divorce

Divorce represents the failure of our most cherished hopes and dreams. It carries with it an enormous sense of loss and disappointment. Even more destructive is the anger that is inevitable as a marriage dissolves. Yet in spite of its unavoidable hurt, divorce also represents a new beginning, an opportunity to move out of a situation which demanded change and to create a better life.

Memories of the hopes and dreams and love with which we began married life remain with us no matter how the relationship develops as time goes by. Looking back on our experience, we often recall and embellish the good side of events, forgetting what we perceive as failure. At other times, we call to mind only the hurts, only the faults of our partner. Such one-sided views aggravate the sense of disappointment and loss and especially, the anger we feel.

The truth is that divorce is seldom a sudden and unwarranted dissolution of a beautiful relationship, rarely a match doomed to failure. The seeds of a divorce have been present throughout the marriage as has been the potential for growth and problem solving. Day-to-day living, one decision laid upon another, has culminated in a situation that one or both parties no longer finds tenable.

It is also natural to believe that divorce was the other person's fault. In some cases, one party's behavior was so destructive that little could have been done to save the relationship. Even in this type situation, there is a tremendous sense of loss and disappointment. It is the anger, though, that creates the greatest difficulty. Why did we give so much of the love and trust most precious to us to someone who could betray that giving? Why were we so foolish? Why did we accept this treatment for so long? Is this what we deserved?

We have to acknowledge that this failed relationship did not happen to some stranger. We attracted this person. We participated in the development of the relationship. We are partially responsible. Then we must forgive ourselves, accepting that we did the best we knew how to do and remembering that mistakes are the inevitable consequence of being human.

We can soften the anger, loss and disappointment of divorce by dealing realistically with what has hurt us. Once we accept responsibility for our actions and forgive ourselves for our share of the problem, we become open to a better life with a more solid and constructive foundation.

AFFIRMATION

*There is a world of love in and
around me that dissolves past
hurts and gives me the courage
to live a full life.*

*I believe in my essential
loving nature and in my
longing to share love with others.
I accept the loss of cherished
dreams and the disappointment
and anger I have felt, knowing
that the right use of love will
never harm me.*

*The strength of the universe fills
my soul, healing my hurts and
showing the way to a beautiful
and loving tomorrow.*

One Second of Sunshine

One second of sunshine
reaches
tentatively
to touch the face
of pain

holding it
in fleeting caress

lifting its gaze
to new life

drawing from strife
what is good.

The Sensations of Life

The sounds, smells and touch of the world around us have tremendous power to heal and to enrich our lives. Yet the sensations of life are translated into our existence only to the extent that we are willing to receive them.

Our inner selves take in the beauty of the world around us when we take the time and energy to open ourselves to the sensual experiences that surround us. If we never open the window, we will never hear the birds sing. If sitting by a fire on a dreary day lifts our spirits, we need to carry in the wood. Yet doing what is necessary to fully experience the sensations of life is usually a pleasure in itself, as what we are about to feel, in anticipation, already exists in our minds.

One of the most soothing and satisfying experiences we can choose to enjoy is music. As we allow ourselves to become absorbed in musical energies, time flows by unnoticed, and the beauty of the universe becomes a part of our being. The stronger our focus on the sounds, the more powerful the reaction. We can feel our internal response. Our hearts expand, in thought, in remembered loss, in sheer joy. But it is all healing.

There are also comforting sounds and smells around us every day. We know most meals in preparation smell good. The more we focus on the pleasure of it, the more it enriches our spirit. And there is the accompanying clatter of dishes, running water, children wanting to know if "it's ready yet." These are all simple and lovely smells and sounds of daily life. As we take them for ourselves, sensing the life and love behind them, the joy is ours.

Each day holds endless opportunities to reach out to the comfort and pleasures of touch. We choose fabrics that feel good, but seldom focus on the sensations of feeling them—soft sheets and towels, dry clothes after a swim, a comfortable couch for a nap. Our lives are filled with people, young and old, who would happily enrich our lives with a hug. The world provides an endless supply of "touchables" for our fulfillment, and so close to our reach, like taking someone's hand.

We determine how we relate to the world around us. As we make a conscious effort to enjoy all that is given freely by humanity and nature, our lives will be rich beyond belief. We have only to focus on the sensations of the things we love.

AFFIRMATION

*The sounds, smells and touch
of the universe reach to me and
enrich my spirit.*

*I rejoice in the sweetness of
a remembered melody and in
natural sounds like falling rain.*

*I love scented spring mornings
and the freshness of air filled
with falling snow.*

*I enjoy the sensations of daily
life- children laughing, kitchen
stoves filling the air with steam.*

*I take to my heart the richness of
the universe that surrounds me.*

Nature's Arms

This morning I awoke in Nature's arms
as she hummed a comforting strain.

Her shoulders muscled in grass-filled hillock
had softened where we'd lain.

And lilac dew, our morning brew,
quickened sleepy hearts

As limbs entwined all through the night
stretched and drew apart.

23 The Necessity of Loss

Loss is an essential part of life. It is necessary to growth. It also deepens our spiritual potential, increasing the ability to experience all aspects of life. The pain of loss can be born with grace when we remember that it is an integral part of the universal whole, whose central urge is the greater good of all humankind.

Watching autumn leaves go through the natural process of change, slipping away to make way for new life, provides inspiration and instruction for humanity. We feel the intense beauty of color, vibrant individual bursts, blending to form a fabulous whole. We watch the breezes carry leaves through the air to end as masses of ground color, joy for childish enthusiasm, beauty for all ages.

Thus it can be for humankind. Letting go of what can no longer give vitality to our lives lends us a special beauty, a richness and vibrancy that arises from a sense of oneness with oneself. When we let go of the need to sustain what has lost its life force for us, we can open ourselves to new experience. Without the need to reach continually to what was the sun and seed of our lives, we once again become part of the free flow of life, part of the graceful movement from old to new, from loss to fulfillment.

Learning to deal with loss is the means through which each of us can realize our full potential. The grandeur of human life lies in its ability to triumph over the challenges that inevitably lie in our path. We learn depth and sensibility through love, courage and personal endurance in the face of the obstacles before us.

It is also in learning to accept loss that we find the kind of love that we seek most in life. In shared loss, our relationships gain depth as we aid each other through difficulties. The only thing that binds more than laughter is the warmth of comfort in times of tears. When we take someone's hand to share and understand their pain, we are intertwining our spirits. When we give warmth to a person feeling loss, we are tacitly accepting that loss with them, and we are helping them to do the same.

Out of pain comes the grandeur of human existence. Out of loss comes the acceptance of possibility and a belief in our own potential as part of a creative universe. Out of shared suffering come loving bonds unmatched by any other. The most beautiful of spirits is one who has faced loss with grace and love and hope for the future of all humankind.

AFFIRMATION

I am part of a universe which is continually renewing itself. Understanding the vitality of all existence, I find the courage to leave behind what is complete.

I feel compassion for the losses of others, as I do for my own. Strength comes to me from the love we share in the process of letting go. We are all one with the universe.

I accept that in order to grow I must release what is no longer fruitful in my life. I accept the loss of what I once needed knowing that this makes possible all new things.

A New Season

Ferns greened with fresh air and life
retreat with me, within
remembering summer's sweetness and song.

Now we view the world
from the same sheltered place,
watching windowed mists
skim cooled waters
as passing birds arch
in effortless grace,
seeking a new home for a calmer life,
a new world far from our sight.

How lovely to hold what summer held,
glorious June days and hot summer nights,
as we look upon a new season.

94 Dealing with Death

Serenity is rooted in acceptance of the essential goodness of the universe. Nothing challenges such a philosophy more than the death of someone we love. Yet only when we view the world in this perspective can we accept loss. There are two truths that enable us to continue to believe in the fundamental goodness of life even in the face of death: first, that there is reality beyond the observable facts of our existence, and second, that we never lose the power to hold in our hearts the essence of whomever we love.

Children react to death from an entirely personal and immediate standpoint. If there is a loss of someone upon whom young people are dependent, they feel total devastation. Facing a problem for which they are almost completely unprepared seems impossible. Only when we come to hold a broad perspective of existence can we accept death with equanimity. Only then can we look beyond the present circumstance and find peace.

We are part of a comprehensive reality that links us with the world around us and goes beyond the objective facts of our existence. The external or physical aspect of our lives is only one manifestation of our essentially spiritual being. Life experience, with its moments of connection to a power greater than ourselves, leads us to conclude this must be so. And we know that even in death, the spirit of those we have loved continues to live as part of us and of every aspect of life they have known. This gives us confidence that, like all spiritual realities, they exist at a level beyond our grasp.

We can also find consolation and hope in the realization that within each spiritual being lies the power to nourish and maintain love for someone who is no longer physically present in our lives. Parents who are separated from their children feel no lessening of affection and care. Friends separated by decades often feel a sense of not having been apart at all at the time of a reunion. Once loving ties have been created, each consciousness has the ability to sustain these feelings. Remembrances of happy times, of problems overcome, of gestures of affection—all such thoughts give life to the love we carry with us. And why should they not be carried in the same way within the spirit of those we have loved?

We live in a universe that holds truths far beyond our understanding. Yet we can come to understand that each spirit continues to exist on many levels even after death. We take comfort in knowing that all those who have touched us continue to live as part of what we are. In this way we can accept the process of dying. The love we hold within lets us turn from our loss, bringing new life to days and, one day, sweet dreams.

AFFIRMATION

The universe embraces every spirit that I love, uniting me with all existence as part of a divine whole.

I open my mind and heart to the inner knowing that teaches me to accept the passing of life into another plane of existence. I listen to the lessons of an understanding greater than myself and learn that life reaches beyond the realities we know.

The higher power that comforts me is a reality beyond this level of existence. Its loving embrace reaches to every spirit and brings us peace.

96

Past Joys Walk
with Him

Part of life left him
on the brightest of days
and rain-filled nights
flowed into the coolness of dawn

Till lost life could touch him
in the deepest of dreams
and feel him respond
in gentle farewell.

Then past joys walked with him
away from the loss
bringing new life to day
love's quiet and sweet dreams.

25 The Love of Life

Nature can feed our spiritual selves. But there are obstacles to opening ourselves to its healing power. All kinds of fears and anxieties keep us from responding to the comfort we need to live life well. We must make a conscious effort to draw on the power of the natural world to restore and nurture the human heart.

Think back to times in your life when you felt very close to nature and experienced its soothing qualities. Generally people recall vacations at the beach or excursions to secluded spots. Most of us have also known private moments of calm in a natural setting at home or insightful spurts of happiness when, upon experiencing some form of natural beauty, we felt an overpowering oneness with the divine.

While we treasure the beauty of such moments, it is important to be able to expand them to times in our daily lives when comfort is most needed. What keeps us from opening ourselves to natural beauty on a regular basis? Why do we rarely turn to the comforts of the natural world when we are plagued by worries and trying to deal with problems? Because we fear the vulnerability involved in an opening of the heart. When we are in trouble, we feel the greatest need to be in control. Yet a mind open to contemplation and feeling has at least momentarily abdicated control.

Opening ourselves to nature is an emotional rather than an intellectual experience. It is comparable to allowing ourselves to care, to love, to be excited. How dangerous these emotions can seem. When we care, we can try and fail. When we love, we can be rejected. When we become excited, we can play the fool. In fact, allowing ourselves to feel deeply can be considered foolish in the adult world. How many of us have fallen into the safe haven of telling ourselves we no longer care about doing our best on the job, reading books that expand our horizons, attempting to help others in need?

To avoid the risks of openings of the heart, we employ powerful rationalizations. We cannot sit quietly in the yard because we have important things to do. We cannot take a solitary walk in the woods because that would be selfish. We do not open the windows on beautiful days because the furniture will get dusty. We lose sight of what we need most.

Such defensive thinking keeps us from the closeness with nature necessary to a life well lived. The problems and stresses of life must be counterbalanced by soothing and strengthening forces, and one of the greatest of these is the beauty nature has to offer. When we open our hearts to life, it will in turn feed us with the sustenance our hearts desire.

AFFIRMATION

The natural beauty of the universe enriches my life, bringing joy and comfort in times of need.

It is my nature to make the quiet beauty of the morning a part of myself. My heart responds to the natural world – sunlight sifting through trees, the smell of the air's freshness, the music of birdsong. I take the freedom and joy of it and accept it as part of myself.

I am the quiet morning. I am the seedbed of growth awaiting the opportunities of the day. I am one with the universe.

Dare I Lay Out My Heart ?

Dare I lay out my heart
to all life

And be loved in return
as its young

Be cradled
in birdsong

Soothed
by sunshine

Lulled by
the harmonies
of night?

Dare I lay out my heart
to love me?

26 **Healing Our Bodies**

Staying healthy is a matter of calming the body and spirit so that the natural harmonies of the universe can function. The stress-inducing emotions – fear, anger, hatred – cause feverish activity in the physical system and induce disease. By learning to draw upon the calming and harmonious universal order, we can maintain the healthy bodies we are intended to enjoy.

The first step to good health is to recognize when the way we respond to our experience is harmful. Dealing with traffic provides a good example. When someone stops short in front of us, it is easy to get hostile. We can let the body join in with angry gestures and full mobilization of our adrenaline resources. We can shout and curse. In fact, there is almost no end to the turmoil we can develop in our minds and bodies. How many of us coolly consider what might have caused the problem? How many quickly reject the idea of a personal affront?

If we wish to do so, we can look within and feel what angry reactions do to the physical system. Every molecule in our being seems to be racing, frantically rushing to a goal not yet in sight. It is as if all inside us is going in different directions with collision imminent. Natural harmony, the easy flow of life-giving breath and blood, is interrupted. We feel out of control.

While such reactions are a necessary part of life, habitual negative thinking is damaging to our health. How long after a trying moment in traffic does it take us to regain our calm? How long is it before our blood pressure and breathing return to normal? Do we generally keep anger in our minds, going over and over the cause of the upset? When our reaction to life's irritations causes lasting turmoil in our systems, we are literally making ourselves ill.

There are countless ways to regain the mental and emotional calm that allows the body to function naturally. But the simplest and most generally useful technique for calming the mind and body is deep breathing. When we break away from a frantic mental state, drawing in long breaths and exhaling slowly, the calming effect is startling. It is even more effective if we focus on the thought of drawing strength from the divine order that surrounds us and then releasing the fear and disorder we are feeling inside.

The natural order of the universe is in and all around us. We have only to draw on its strength, breathing into our lives the harmony that leads to vibrant health, releasing the negative thinking that is damaging to body and soul. We can make a conscious choice to sustain the calm that brings us the mental and physical health we desire.

AFFIRMATION

The universe is a healthy system that functions harmoniously. My mind and body are part of this universal order. It is my nature to be healthy.

I hold in my mind the harmonies of the healthy life I desire, replacing negative thinking with a peaceful consciousness that allows my body to function smoothly.

My body, mind and universal order are one. I breathe into my being the divinity that surrounds me, bringing life to my life and calm to body and soul.

Harmonies

She takes the quiet sounds
draws them in with her breath
listening, intent
for the song
that stills fear.

She takes the calming air
breathing into her life
harmonies
and draws on the strength
that heals hurt.

She holds the breath of life
lets it into her soul
sensing her oneness
with the healing whole

And breathes through her being
the music of life
of quiet order
and comfort
healing body and soul.

The Unity of Life

We have all opened our hearts to the peace and harmony of the natural world around us. Our memories remind us that the capacity to reach to the natural world for the comfort and strength we need to live life well exists at the heart of all of us. Sharing natural life satisfies the soul and we suffer when we are separated from this source of joy and strength.

Children instinctively know that nature provides what heals as well as what brings comfort and satisfaction to the mind and heart. They long to be outside, feeling the freeness of it, the opportunity for the spirit to roam, to find new excitements and treasures. What they also need is the freshness of the air, the sunlight glowing through trees, the hills to climb. They are drawing to themselves the sustenance of their souls.

As adults, we often lose sight of the good children naturally seek. We worry about what needs to be accomplished, what we must feverishly control. The letting-go of a youthful spirit seems very far away, the opening of the mind and heart to the simple beauties of the world around us no longer a natural function of life. Doing the laundry or working overtime seems more adult and valuable than a walk in the woods. We often genuinely believe that "there is no time."

Yet there is a longing in all humankind for an intimacy between our own divine nature and the divinity in the world around us. Ralph Waldo Emerson so beautifully presented this point of view in his 19th century essays. He saw all life as part of a single whole, believing that man, nature and divinity are inextricably bound. Thus the ability of nature to enrich our lives is founded in the truth that nature, God and humanity are one.

Our own experience shows us that universal power permeates all existence. To grow and to heal are the nature of life. We share that natural right. To bring into our lives all the good we desire, we have only to create an opening in our deepest selves. And one of the best ways to do this is to allow ourselves to experience the comfort and inspiration of natural beauty.

We all seek the communion of the divinity that exists both in us and in the world we share. As we become closer to the life of the universe, we feel its tremendous healing potential for our inner selves. Believing in the unity and in the essential goodness of life, we can reach to the power in ourselves and in the world around us to create lives that reflect our divine intention.

AFFIRMATION

There is a power in the universe that enriches my life. Its energy is in and all around me, filling my life with its strength.

I make the effort to expand my connection with the divinity of the universe, accepting and appreciating the beauty and the nourishing force of the natural world around me.

As I feel the unity of the power that exists in me and in the world around me, I learn to create a life filled with the harmony and peace I desire.